W9-BLX-693

David Suzuki

Bryan Pezzi

Weigl

Published by Weigl Educational Publishers Limited
6325 10th Street S.E.
Calgary, Alberta T2H 2Z9
Website: www.weigl.com

Library and Archives Canada Cataloguing-in-Publication Data available upon request.
Fax (403) 233-7769 for the attention of the Publishing Records department.

ISBN 978-1-77071-595-0 (hard cover)
ISBN 978-1-77071-601-8 (soft cover)

Printed in the United States of America in North Mankato, Minnesota
1 2 3 4 5 6 7 8 9 0 14 13 12 11 10

072010
WEP230610

Editor: Aaron Carr   **Design:** Kenzie Browne

All of the Internet URLs given in the book were valid at the time of publication. However, due to the dynamic nature of the Internet, some addresses may have changed, or sites may have ceased to exist since publication. While the author and publisher regret any inconvenience this may cause readers, no responsibility for any such changes can be accepted by either the author or the publisher.

We gratefully acknowledge the financial support of the Government of Canada through the Canada Book Fund for our publishing activities.

Photo Credits
CP (Fred Chartrand): page 3 bottom, 16; CP (Tim Krochak): page 5; CP (Jack Long): pages 10-11; CP (Larry MacDougal): page 1; Getty Images: pages 17 top, 17 bottom, 18, 19 top, 19 middle, 19 bottom, 22 right; courtesy of David Suzuki: pages 3 top, 8, 9, 13, 14 bottom, 15 top.

Every reasonable effort has been made to trace ownership and to obtain permission to reprint copyright material. The publishers would be pleased to have any errors or omissions brought to their attention so that they may be corrected in subsequent printings.

CONTENTS

Who is David Suzuki?

Dr. David Suzuki is a scientist. He is best-known for hosting the successful television show *The Nature of Things*. On the show, Suzuki explains science in a way that is fun and easy to learn.

Suzuki also teaches people about the environment. In 1990, he started the David Suzuki Foundation with his wife, Dr. Tara Cullis. This group works to protect nature.

Suzuki has written many newspaper stories. He also hosts radio shows about science.

Growing Up

On March 24, 1936, David Takayoshi Suzuki was born in Vancouver, British Columbia. Suzuki's parents ran a dry cleaning shop. His family lived in an apartment in the back of the shop. Suzuki has a twin sister and two younger sisters.

Suzuki loved nature from an early age. He liked to fish and explore forests and lakes with his father. Sometimes, Suzuki collected insects and made displays of them. When Suzuki was nine years old, his family moved to Ontario. There, he explored the nature of Point Pelee National Park and the swamps near his home.

British Columbia, Home of David Suzuki

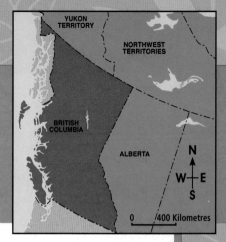

- Suzuki lives and works in Vancouver.
- Vancouver is the largest city in the province. There are more than two million people living in the Vancouver area.
- For 38 years, Suzuki worked as a professor of **zoology** at the University of British Columbia.
- British Columbia is bordered by the Pacific Ocean on the west coast.
- The province is home to some of the largest and oldest trees in the world.

Influences

The greatest influence in Suzuki's life was his father. His father's name was Kaoru, but most people called him Carr.

Carr's parents moved to Canada from Japan before he was born. As a child, Carr learned the Japanese ways of his family. He also learned Canadian ways of life.

Carr taught Suzuki the importance of education. He also supported Suzuki's love of science. Carr even helped Suzuki learn how to speak in public.

Overcoming Obstacles

Suzuki's family is Japanese Canadian. In the 1930s and 1940s, Japanese Canadians were treated poorly in Canada. They could not vote or hold certain jobs.

When Suzuki was six years old, he and his family were forced to move. This happened because Canada was at war with Japan. All Japanese Canadians had to move into **internment camps**. Many Japanese Canadians had to leave their belongings behind. Suzuki's new home was crowded and dirty. There was no school during his first year in the camp. A school was added later.

11

Practice Makes Perfect

Suzuki went to a special school inside the internment camp. He began grade 1 when he was seven years old. Even though Suzuki started late, he did well in school. Suzuki completed grades 1, 2, and 3 in one year.

After the war ended, Suzuki attended public school. He became known as a good student. In grade 10, Suzuki entered his first public speaking contest. He won first prize. After that, Suzuki won many more speaking contests. His public speaking skills helped Suzuki earn a place on his school's student council. Later, Suzuki became president of his high school.

VOTE DAVE SUZUKI FOR PRESIDENT

Key Events

Suzuki first appeared on television in 1962. He was in eight episodes of the University of Alberta show *Your University Speaks*.

In 1968, the Canadian **Broadcasting** Corporation (CBC) asked Suzuki to host a science show. Soon, Suzuki had his own television show called *Suzuki on Science*. In later years, he hosted other television and radio shows.

In 1979, Suzuki began working on *The Nature of Things*. The show has been broadcast weekly on CBC for more than 30 years. It is Canada's longest-running **documentary** television series. *The Nature of Things* has aired in 83 countries.

In 1985, Suzuki worked on a show about the environment. It was called *A Planet for the Taking*. Millions of viewers watched every week. This eight-part **miniseries** won an environmental award from the **United Nations**.

Achievements and Successes

Suzuki earned a doctor of science degree in 1961. Then, he went to work at the University of British Columbia. There, Suzuki ran the biggest **genetics** lab in Canada. Suzuki won an award for being the best Canadian scientist under the age of 35. He won this award three years in a row.

In 1986, the United Nations gave Suzuki an award for helping people understand science. In 2006, he was named a Companion of the **Order of Canada**. This is the highest award a Canadian citizen can receive.

Suzuki holds 24 **honourary degrees** from universities around the world.

His work in television has won four **Gemini Awards** and received praise around the world. In 2002, Suzuki won the John Drainie Award. This award is for broadcasting excellence.

Suzuki has written 48 books. Of these, 19 are science books for children.

In 2009, Suzuki won the Right Livelihood Award. He was given this award for his lifetime of work in science.

What is a Scientist?

A scientist is a person who studies the natural world. There are many kinds of scientists. Most scientists spend much of their time doing research. They ask questions about nature and then try to find answers. Some scientists try to cure illnesses. Other scientists make inventions that improve people's lives.

Suzuki is a special kind of scientist. He is a geneticist. A geneticist is a scientist who studies genes. A gene is part of a code found inside the **cells** of all living things. This code gives animals and plants their **traits**.

Scientists Through History

Like Suzuki, these scientists have achieved success in their field of study.

Sir Frederick Banting

Banting studied medicine. With the help of his partner, Charles Best, he discovered insulin. People with a disease called diabetes use insulin to stay healthy.

Biruté Galdikas

Galdikas studies large apes called orangutans. Orangutans live in rain forests. Galdikas studies these animals in their natural **habitat**. She has won many awards for her work.

Roberta Bondar

Bondar studies how the human brain works with the eyes so that people can see. She is also Canada's first female astronaut. In 1992, Bondar flew on the space shuttle *Discovery*. She studied how the human body works in space.

Timeline

1936 | David Takayoshi Suzuki is born on March 24 in Vancouver.

1942 | Suzuki and his family are sent to live in an internment camp.

1958 | Suzuki graduates from Amherst College with an honours degree in science.

1961 | The University of Chicago grants Suzuki a doctor of science degree.

1962	Suzuki appears on television for the first time.
1979	*The Nature of Things* airs on CBC for the first time.
1985	Suzuki's show, *A Planet for the Taking,* wins an award from the United Nations.
1990	Suzuki and his wife, Dr. Tara Cullis, start the David Suzuki Foundation.
2004	CBC viewers choose Suzuki as one of the 10 greatest Canadians.
2006	Suzuki is named Companion of the Order of Canada.

Write a Biography

A person's life story can be the subject of a book. This kind of book is called a biography. Biographies describe the lives of people who have had great success or done important things to help others. These people may be alive today, or they may have lived many years ago.

Try writing your own biography. First, decide who you want to write about. You can choose a scientist, such as David Suzuki, or any other person you find interesting.

Then, find out if your library has any books about this person. Write down the key events in this person's life.

- What was this person's childhood like?
- What has he or she accomplished?
- What are his or her goals?
- What makes this person special or unusual?

Answer the questions in your notebook. Your answers will help you write a biography.

Find Out More

To learn more about David Suzuki, visit these websites.

Learn about the David Suzuki Foundation at this site.
www.davidsuzuki.org

Read more about Canadian science and scientists at this site.
www.science.ca

Learn more about Suzuki's show, *The Nature of Things*, at this site.
www.cbc.ca/documentaries/natureofthings

Find out how you can help the environment at this site.
www.nrdc.org/reference/kids.asp

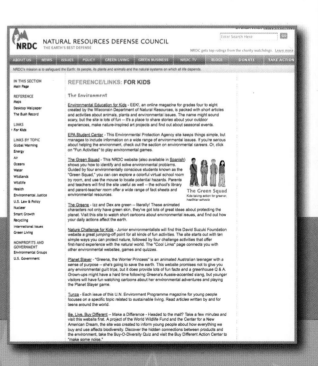

Glossary

broadcasting: airing programs on television or radio

cells: the smallest parts of any living thing

documentary: a television show or movie that is based on facts

Gemini Awards: annual awards given for excellence in Canadian television and movies

genetics: the study of genes; the code inside cells that gives living things their special features

habitat: the environment where an animal or plant makes its home

honourary degrees: university degrees given to a person in honour of his or her acheivements

internment camps: places where certain groups of people are held when a country is at war

miniseries: a television show made up of a small number of episodes

Order of Canada: a special award for Canadians who have made a major difference to Canada

traits: qualities that make one kind of plant or animal different from another

United Nations: an organization made up of most of the countries in the world

zoology: the study of animals

Index